A group of typical thatched-cottage pastille burners of the 1830s.

Porcelain Pastille Burners

Robert Devereux and Vega Wilkinson

A Shire b

D1158590

Published in 2005 by Shire Publications Ltd,
Cromwell House, Church Street, Princes Risborough,
Buckinghamshire HP27 9AA, UK.
(Website: www.shirebooks.co.uk)

British Library Cataloguing in Publication Data:
Devereux, Robert
Porcelain pastille burners. – (Shire album; 439)
1. Porcelain 2. Incense burners and containers
I. Title II. Wilkinson, Vega
738.2'8
ISBN 0 7478 0622 5

Cover: *A white Gothic pavilion, c.1830, no marks but possibly by Alcock. (H 18.5, W 17, D 12.5.)*
A candle was placed in this pastille burner to show how it would look when used as a night-light.

NOTE: Where the size of the pastille burners illustrated is given, measurements are in
centimetres. H = height, W = width and D = depth.

ACKNOWLEDGEMENTS
We wish to thank Rodney and Eileen Hampson for their invaluable help and
encouragement throughout this project; Gaye Blake Roberts, Curator of the Wedgwood
Museum, and Lynn Miller, Information Officer at the Wedgwood Museum; Audrey
Dudson of the Dudson Museum, who helped to identify hitherto-unknown Dudson
examples; Miranda Goodby, Curator of Ceramics at the Potteries Museum and Art
Gallery, Stoke-on-Trent; Alan Finney of the Ceramic Restoration Studios, Biddulph, for his
research on the Dudson cottages. Tree-harvest (6 The Hawthorns, Hawthorn Lane,
Corse, Gloucestershire GL19 3NY; telephone: 01452 849123; website: www.tree-
harvest.com) supplied all the ingredients for the pastilles and pomanders we made. Any
publication relies first and foremost on its pictures and Martin Greatbach ABIPP of Brown
Edge, Stoke-on-Trent, was responsible for the photography, providing new ideas with
which to represent this fascinating subject. Finally, thanks go to Chris Jowitt of Warner
Antiques, Brasted, Kent, for finding many of the cottages and castles illustrated, and to
Olwen Grant, whose patience and editorial skills have been essential.

Printed in Great Britain by CIT Printing Services, Press Buildings, Merlins Bridge,
Haverfordwest, Pembrokeshire SA61 1XF.

Contents

A Chinese temple, c.1840, by an unknown maker. (H 15.5, W 16, D 13.5.)

Pastille burners: an overview

Pastille burners are ornamental objects suitable for holding a burning scented pastille. In the eighteenth and early nineteenth centuries they were an important part of every household, used to counteract the unpleasant smells associated with poor personal hygiene, smoke from burning candles and the lack of sanitation in villages and towns.

The art of perfumery was well established in the earliest civilisations of both Egypt and China and recipes for perfumes, with many samples, have been found in Egyptian tombs dating before 3000 BC. The art was continued by the Greeks and Romans. During the sixteenth century a range of scented materials was brought into Europe from the Levant. In Elizabethan England floors were covered with dried flowers and herbs such as lavender, sweet flag and bay, sometimes up to a foot deep, which were replaced when the smell became unbearable. Wealthy households had their own still-rooms where the mistress of the house created dry and wet pot-pourri from dried flowers and essential oils, which she put into large, beautiful containers made of bronze. One sixteenth-century Ming dynasty bronze and enamelled incense burner was modelled in the shape of a duck. It measured 28 cm high and stood on a plinth, and the perfumed smoke poured from the duck's open beak. With the introduction of porcelain, a much wider range of vessels began to be produced in the late eighteenth century. Their shapes and patterns were often based on Chinese pieces that had been brought to Britain by the Honourable East India Company. At the same time, in Germany, the Meissen and Dresden factories were producing fine pastille burners.

Above and right: An unusual, large house, c. 1835, attributed to Alcock. There is a central well with a pierced cover to hold either pastilles or pomanders. (H 25.5, W 26, D 18.5.)

A rare, large Georgian house, c.1825, attributed to Alcock. The back of the base is unusual, being pierced with fifteen holes to increase the draught and allow the perfume from the pastille burner to escape freely. (H 20.5, W 26, D 25.)

By 1800 the Wedgwood pottery was producing a full range of large and small incense burners and pot-pourri holders. They were made from black basalt and decorated with neo-classical designs and painted enamels. The Wedgwood shape book shows many small baskets and incense burners of various shapes and sizes priced around six shillings. They are very similar to those in the Spode shape book of the same period except that Wedgwood was making them in black basalt and Spode in the new body, bone china. The potteries catered for members of the aristocracy and the wealthy upper class such as Lady Granville, the wife of the British ambassador in Turkey, who in 1836 received a gift of gilt and brown pastilles from the Turkish ambassador, a most suitable gift at this time. These pastilles were small blocks or cones of charcoal dipped in fragrant oils and were meant to be burnt. The pastille was placed inside the burner in various ways, usually by lifting the cottage off the base, lifting the roof, inserting it through an aperture at the back, or with a slide. The pastille was then lit with a spill. The burners were designed to be placed in any room of the house. The Swansea pottery also made basalt burners; one, in the shape of a vase decorated with moulded neo-classical allegorical figures, is thought to have been made *c*.1805 to commemorate the death of Nelson.

In the nineteenth century, when British potters had discovered the secret of bone china, the range became much larger. Beautifully decorated pot-pourri jars and incense burners were designed by some of the well-known potters such as Josiah Spode and by many smaller Staffordshire potteries. They were still often decorated with designs of Chinese or Japanese influence.

The fashion for burning pastilles in decorative holders spread from the aristocracy to the emerging affluent middle classes throughout Britain in the first half of the nineteenth century. Ceramic cottages had already been produced in the 1750s; two were

A Chinoiserie pavilion, c.1840, by an unknown maker. The roof is detachable. (H 18.5, W 13, D 11.5.)

mentioned in a sixteen-day sale at the Chelsea pottery held in 1756. It was not until the 1820s, however, that the master potters started to produce a small range of a size and shape aimed at middle-class customers. The designs are fascinating: pastille burners were produced in the shapes of castles, churches, lodges, tollhouses and gazebos or summerhouses, as well as large and small cottages. Some had detachable roofs or bases, or slides, which were all designed for easy access to place and light the pastilles. For over fifty years these

A rare gabled house, possibly by Spode. (H 11, W 13, D 13.)

Above left: *A stylised lavender model of Warwick Castle, c.1825, possibly by Alcock. (H 15.5, W 14, D 14.)*
Above right: *This popular castle was later used as an ornament.*

elegant pastille burners reflected the architecture of Regency and Victorian Britain.

The Victorian middle-class housewife began to collect more and more furniture, wall hangings and ornaments, reflecting the tastes of her social class. She saw her house as a place of refuge from the grime and poverty found in the streets and favoured objects with a

Above left: *An unusual cottage, c.1820, marked '1142' in purple and painted 'D'. The maker is unknown. (H 9, W 6, D 6.)*
Above right: *A small square cottage with a thatched roof. Although there are no marks, it is attributed to Worcester. (H 8, W 7, D 7.)*

A biscuit church with a nave and tower and roof pinnacles, by an unknown maker. (H 17, W 14.5, D 12.)

A double-fronted, two-piece house, c.1820, possibly made by Grainger of Worcester. (H 12.5, W 13.5, D 12.)

more rural charm. The Victorians firmly believed that polluted air was the cause of much of the disease that led to such a high mortality rate; the average life span of gentlefolk was only forty-four years and that of workers twenty-two. In contrast to the conditions of the towns and cities the countryside was seen as a safer, more wholesome place. Romantic poets and artists idealised the countryside and helped make the rural idyll popular. Pastille burners at this time served a dual purpose: they appeared to combat disease by keeping the air sweet and, in their varying and colourful designs, reflected the personal taste of the lady of the house.

A biscuit two-storey house, c.1820, marked on the pastille slide 'Chamberlains Royal porcelain'. (H 14,W 14, D 14.)

A blue dovecote, c.1830, by Dudson. (H 13.5, W 11.5, D 11.5.)

An octagonal keep, c.1830, by Alcock, also made in lavender. (H 13.5, W 12.5, D 12.5.)

Each pottery soon claimed its own niche in the market. The pastille burners of Chamberlains of Worcester were the most elaborate. Spode offered a range of large and small gazebos, their finest being a Swiss house, while the Coalport pottery produced similar summerhouses and rustic cottages. Neither Derby nor Minton seemed to be interested in this market, each producing a very small range; only two Derby burners are known. Two men in particular, Samuel Alcock at the Hill Top pottery, Burslem, and Thomas Dudson at the Hope Street pottery, Hanley, created a vast range of designs and sizes suitable for any room in the house. The pastille burners were hand-painted and the porcelain flowers with which many of the cottages are decorated reflect the growing interest in plants and the importance of the garden.

A unique octagonal tower (left), c.1830, by an unknown maker, and (right) the base of the tower. (H 14, W 12.5, D 12.5.)

By the middle of the nineteenth century sanitation and hygiene had improved. Water closets came into general use and, following the discovery that cholera and typhoid, two of the major threats to the population, were spread by polluted well water, pure running water was available from taps in the house by the late 1860s.

Despite these improvements, fragrant pastilles were still needed in most homes. Candles, which had first been home-made from tallow (melted-down mutton fat) and gave off a pungent smell when lit,

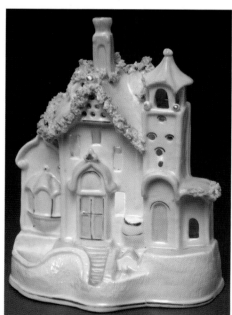

were now being commercially produced from beeswax. By the eighteenth century a profitable urban trade had evolved and candles were sold in varying sizes and attractively packaged. They were, however, expensive. By the 1830s a French chemist, Michel Chevreul, had discovered how to extract stearin from sperm oil. The process, known as 'saponification', was patented by the British firm of Edward Price & Company, which began producing candles made from stearin and eventually from coconut and palm oil. Although the middle classes were now able to afford these more fragrant, white candles for their public rooms when entertaining, their servants still had tallow candles and in some cases rush lights. When candles in guest bedrooms were replaced with the old smelly tallow ones it was time for the guests to leave.

A folly, c.1840, with a night-light. The maker is unknown. (H 17, W 13.5, D 7.8.)

Dudson pot-pourri, c.1880. Terracotta body decorated with Jackfield-type glaze. Courtesy of Dudson Museum.

Even after gaslight and oil lamps had replaced candles, pastille burners were still needed. At first gas lighting was very smelly. In 1824 William Bailey the younger patented a Gas Consumer, for 'consuming' the smoke from gas burners and lamps, but there is no record of how successful it was, and Bailey & Batkin of Longton, Staffordshire, produced a Perdifume of red earthenware. At a little over 22 cm (8³/₄ inches) high, it was surmounted by a lion and leaves and decorated all over with silver lustre. The Perdifume was also supposedly able to consume gas and lamp smoke.

Some of the larger, more robust pastille burners were marketed to be used also as night-lights. Night-light candles, described as small cylinders of wax in a paper or metal container, did not strictly need a holder but were often hidden in special porcelain containers.

White and coloured garden pavilions, c.1830, possibly by Alcock. (H 18,W 17, D 12.5.)

A tall, white house, c. 1830, by an unknown maker. (H 11, W 7.2, D 7.2.)

Grainger of Worcester marketed a tall house for this purpose and many of both the Alcock and Dudson ranges would have been suitable.

By the 1860s pastille burners had became purely ornamental. The cottages still came in a variety of shapes and designs but the various openings for the pastilles, now no longer needed, were omitted. Some of the castle shapes became adapted for use as money-boxes. The popularity of the cottages, however, was such that they continued to be found in all classes of Victorian homes.

The *Illustrated London News* of 19th September 1936 included an article entitled 'A Page for Collectors: A China Village'. Captain D. N. Whitacker had advised an American collector on the creation of a miniature village on a painted plaster model. Many makers of pastille burners are represented in the model. The animals and human figures, which helped to create the village scene, were made of glass. The village was lit by electricity. After completion it was taken to the United States on the Cunard vessel *Queen Mary*. The article concludes: 'The village represents a century of experiment by innumerable potters, most of them nameless, and is thus not just an amusing and elaborate toy but an authentic cross-section of history.'

This porcelain 'village' represents a century of experiment by innumerable potters. (Photograph from 'Illustrated London News', 19th September 1936.)

Sources of design

Master potters, designers and modellers have always been influenced by the fashions of the day. Their travelling representatives were in direct contact with all levels of society and brought ideas for new designs and products back to the pottery. By the beginning of the nineteenth century designs were available for a new and fashionable project, the picturesque village.

Regency England was developing rapidly; the country house became a status symbol reflecting its owner's power, wealth and taste. Designs for country estates were influenced by the ideas of

Lancelot 'Capability' Brown (1716–83) and landowners and their families delighted in the open aspect of the rolling countryside that Brown had created for them. Summerhouses, follies, pagodas, temples and dovecotes dotted these parkland estates.

The picturesque style of an ornately decorated individual, pretty cottage, known as *cottage orné*, was in vogue in Britain. William Gilpin (1724–1804), a clergyman, artist and author of *Picturesque Tours of the 1770s*, was probably the first writer to theorise on

Left: *A large two-storey mansion, c.1825, with pastille slide, possibly by Alcock. (H 16.5, W 20, D 19.5.)*

Far left: *A hexagonal pavilion, c.1835, used as either a pastille burner or a night-light, possibly by Alcock. (H 22.5, W 18.5, D 17.)*

Left: *A slightly smaller white undecorated model.*

A cottage house, c.1830, by an unknown maker. Note the bird on the dormer window. (H 13, W 10.5, D 10.)

the picturesque style. Sir Uvedale Price, in an essay published in 1790, described the picturesque village as having intricacy, variety and a play of outline, which could be achieved by the use of colour washes, the addition of overhanging thatched eaves and in particular the use of intricate and large chimneys.

Picturesque cottages were surrounded by a garden planted with lush vegetation and creepers curling up the walls. Landowners had derelict dwellings near to their country houses demolished and replaced with these charming cottages.

This style can be found in the pastille burners produced at the time, notably those of the Spode and Chamberlain potteries. In the late eighteenth century many pattern books and engravings were produced by architects and builders such as Nathaniel Kent. In 1775 he produced a pattern book entitled *Hints to Gentlemen of the Landed Gentry*. John Claudius Loudon wrote the *Encyclopedia of Cottage, Farm and Village Architecture* in 1836 with a supplement in 1842. Master potters and their designers drew on source material such as these publications.

The first picturesque village was built at Blaise Hamlet near Bristol in 1810. Although Sir Uvedale Price had advocated variety in

A cottage, possibly a small lodge house, c.1840, made by Alcock. The door forms a slide for the pastille. (H 12.5, W 17.5, D 16.5.)

villages in 1790, cottages of different designs had not previously been erected together. A Quaker banker named John Scandrett Harford commissioned John Nash (1752–1835) to design cottages around a village green. Harford and Nash had worked together previously in 1802 to design a thatched dairy house in the grounds of Blaise Castle. The new village, Blaise Hamlet, typified the true meaning of picturesque and became a popular excursion from Clifton and Bristol for visiting artists. A series of lithographs was published in 1826 with an introduction describing the different features to be seen at Blaise Hamlet and recommending a visit. In 1814 the *Virtuoso Drawing Magazine* urged its artistic subscribers to draw old cottages with chalk and a milk wash; more skilled artists were then urged to find Gothic lodges to sketch and paint.

The larger country estates had lodges for their gamekeeper and gardener and hunting lodges in which shooting parties were entertained. Small cottages or lodges were built on the approaches leading to the big house; their numbers varied depending on the length of the drive. They were designed with many windows so the gatekeeper could see family guests and visitors approaching. These dwellings usually followed the general architectural design of the main estate.

In the royal parks lodges were of considerable size and provided homes for many important persons. Lord John Russell, for example, lived in Pembroke Lodge in Richmond Park, London, for over thirty years. Windsor Great Park Lodge is another fine example modelled as a pastille burner by permission of Queen Victoria. Some of the

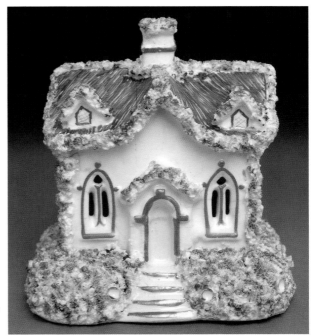

A typical Gothic-style cottage, c.1820, by an unknown maker. (H 10.5, W 10, D 8.5.)

Left and above: *Windsor Lodge,
a seven-galleried mansion, c.1825,
by an unknown maker. (H 15.5,
W 21, D 19.)*

*A lodge with a square tower, c.1830. The tower is
an inkwell with the penholder on one wing with an
opening at the back for the pastille burner, marked
with number 136 on the base. (H 7.5, W 7.5, D 8.)*

*A chapel, c.1830, marked with number 134 on the
base, by an unknown maker. (H 13.5, W 17, D 8.)*

A three-piece, square, ornate house, c.1830, by an unknown maker. (H 16.5, W 14, D 12.5.)

larger rare pastille burners may have been modelled on the villa style of architecture. Originally denoting a Roman farmhouse, the term *villa* came to be used for a country residence, a suitable place in which to retire, again in fine parkland and surrounded by pleasure gardens.

The potters who designed models of these attractive cottages as pastille burners knew that they were providing a functional item that would perfume the house but also never lost sight of their purely decorative appeal. Wherever they were placed in the home, they provided a talking point for friends and guests. Many burners may have been specially commissioned as small replicas of cottages on the estate.

Many pastille burners are in the shape of tollhouses, which had become part of the landscape by the nineteenth century. The most famous one was at Gretna Green, where eloping couples were married by the local blacksmith. A network of turnpike roads was spreading across Britain and Josiah Wedgwood and Josiah Spode, both famous potters, were among the many hundreds of trustees who invested in them. As the conditions of the roads improved, an increasing number of mail- and stage-coach services provided improved communications. By 1838 it was estimated that 7800 tollgates and bars were operational and the road transport system was not fully challenged by the railways until the 1840s. The tollhouses provided living accommodation for the toll-keeper and his family. Early ones were simple in construction but by the 1830s they were far more elaborate in design, with thatched roofs and of various shapes. However, the essential part of their design was purely functional: they had many windows, so the toll-keeper could see all aspects of the road, and porches and overhanging eaves, to protect their occupants from the inclement weather.

An ornate stylised summerhouse by Dudson, c.1830.

Tollhouses by unknown makers, typical of the 1830s: (left) rustic tollhouse (H 12.5, W 11.5, D 11.5); lavender octagonal tollhouse (H 15.5, W 11.5, D 11.5).

Although the individual tastes of the turnpike trustees were reflected in the designs, they generally followed the trend in architectural style and, yet again, provided an ideal source for pottery design. Many of the potteries produced a small range in different sizes and they are hexagonal or octagonal in shape with differing styles of roofs. Tollhouses have been described as umbrella or round thatched cottages.

Dovecotes provided yet another source of design for pastille burners. They were among the many auxiliary buildings on a large country estate, along with the dairy, laundry, ice and turf houses. As early as Roman times pigeons were bred for meat, a practice that continued until the end of the eighteenth century, pigeon pie being often on the menu. Dovecote designs are many. Originally they were built purely for practical purposes and in the local traditional style but by the 1800s their designs fitted architecturally into the overall plan of the estate. Many examples can still be seen in the countryside. The dovecote designed by Sanderson Miller at Wroxton Abbey in Oxfordshire was of one of the features in the park, along with a folly and temple. It has eight sides and is built of stone, with arrow-slit windows.

A Gothic-style dovecote with a bird on the roof, c.1830, by an unknown maker. (H 5, W 9, D 10.)

Above left: *An octagonal lavender tower, c.1830, impressed number 12, by Alcock. (H 14.5, W 12, D 11.) It was possibly modelled on the dovecote at Wroxton Abbey, Oxfordshire.*
Above right: *A pagoda by an unknown maker, c.1840. (H 15, W 12, D 9.)*

Both the summerhouse and the dairy house were used for entertaining visitors to the country estate. The dairy was an important part of the estate. A pretty building, often in a shady part of the grounds, it may have had a porch and a tiled floor; around the room there would have been marble slabs to hold the china cream pots and the walls were often covered with blue and white tiles. The lady of the house took a great interest in both the dairy and the cheese room and they became part of her estate tour. She would take her visitors to the dairy, where they would be offered a drink of milk, served to the aristocracy in fine chinaware but to the gentry in earthenware.

The gazebo or summerhouse was built on a hill overlooking the park, along with Gothic-style temples and Chinese-inspired pagodas, which were all part of the British country house estate. In the 1770s summerhouses were especially popular in Ireland. Peter Somerville-Large wrote in his book *Irish Country Houses*: '... for you must know it is quite the fashion in Ireland to have a cottage neatly fitted out with Tonbridge ware and drink tea in it in the summer.' The family with their visitors or house guests were taken by carriage to one of these

A two-storey lavender pagoda possibly by Alcock, c.1830. (H 16, W 11, D 8.)

Above: *Small cottages by an unknown maker, c.1830, showing the detachable base. (H 8.5, W 10, D 8.5.)*

Left: *A small farm labourer's cottage, c.1830, by an unknown maker. (H 12.5, W 11, D 10.)*

A small castle, possibly a folly, impressed '125', by Alcock. (H 10.5, W 8.5, D 7.)

*A stylised lavender version of Warwick Castle,
c.1830. (H 19, W 19, D 15.5.)*

attractive buildings, where a picnic lunch or afternoon tea would be
served. These small buildings were ideal for pottery designers to
adapt for pastille burners or night-lights. They were often made in a
range of sizes and were some of the most popular designs of the
period.

Follies were also features of the new parkland. It is difficult to
generalise about the influence they had on pastille-burner design
and one can only wonder whether some of the small castle-shaped
burners were modelled on them. Octagonal-shaped pastille burners
may have come from old castle designs as it is thought that part of
Warwick Castle was the subject of some of the burners.

Perfumery

'Perfumery is the art of manipulating odoriferous substances for the gratification of the sense of smell.' (*Encyclopedia Britannica*, ninth edition, 1885)

Since time immemorial man has been aware of the potential of perfume, herbs and spices for many purposes. Early Chinese civilisations used them both medicinally and for creating pleasant environments. In ancient Egypt, Greece and Rome the trade in these substances expanded and the art of perfumery was perfected; it was no longer used only to appease the gods but for personal use as well.

Perfumes were first introduced into Britain by the Romans but their use declined and it was not until the reign of Elizabeth I that they became popular again. Most country gardens had a herb plot, where jonquils, wallflowers, lilac and lavender were grown for making into wet or dry pot-pourri and pomanders. Many new and exciting perfumery imports from the East provided a vast range from which to choose.

It is difficult today to imagine how many unpleasant smells were being produced by a developing society. Each different trade produced its own special odour: the boiling of glue, the brewing of beer, and the making of tallow candles. These, together with the

(Left) A white cottage, c. 1830, with a small slide for the pastille, forming a chimney breast at one end. Although this piece is unmarked it is possibly by Lloyd Shelton. (H 11.5, W 12, D 12.) (Right) A white octagonal tower, c. 1830, possibly from the same pottery as the white cottage. (H 14.5, W 13, D 13.)

smells of rotting vegetables, tobacco, unwashed and unhealthy bodies, not to mention human and animal waste, all entered the home. Even stale perfume would have been unpleasant. However, various traders sold wares intended to suppress or counteract these odours. In the cities and towns apothecaries sold herbs, powders, pills, pomades and love potions. London's apothecaries traded from Camomile Street and Bucklebury Market in Cheapside. They wore black and their shops were distinguished by the symbol of a skull and ancient book in the window. There were also herb dealers, who sold a vast variety of produce, some supplying fresh herbs grown in their own gardens, and perfumiers, who dealt in exotic spices, essential oils, gums and aromatic woods. In the country people could buy from wandering pedlars or at the local country fairs, or they could make their own.

The ladies of the country houses became skilful in the use of herbs to heal many different maladies and made their own pot-pourri, pastilles and pomanders in the still-room. This was usually situated off the housekeeper's room, as its care was one of the housekeeper's duties, and she would have had a still-room maid to assist her. The room was rather like a kitchen, with a fireplace, boiler and sink, and having many shelves and drying surfaces, sometimes even a small bookcase. It was a pleasant, comfortable room, also used as a sitting-room by the female servants. The perfumery and healing recipes were recorded in a 'still book', which was handed down from generation to generation. The recipes became a subject of conversation at social functions held by the lady of the house, who might be persuaded to divulge the secret of the new perfume pervading her house.

Pastilles were easy to make. The base was a finely ground charcoal, often willow because it burns evenly, mixed with saltpetre to assist the burning. Despite the forced draught of the miniature cottages (many of which have holes in the base, open windows and chimneys), the charcoal would go out unless some saltpetre were added. The amount varied according to the nature of the charcoal but was usually about one part of saltpetre to ten to twenty parts of charcoal. Some aromatic resin, such as benzoin, was added to improve the scent; it was ground up and mixed with the charcoal and saltpetre. The mixture needed something to bind it together, usually gum arabic or gum tragacanth, just enough being added to bond the mixture into a stiff dough. Next the chosen essential perfume was added to the mixture. Only a few drops were required. Experiments have shown that lavender, sandalwood, rose, jasmine and cedar wood would all have been suitable but many other aromatic resins and oils were used in old pastille recipes, for example frankincense, myrrh and orris.

The dough was formed into pastilles in a conical mould. The pastilles were left to dry for at least two days and were then ready for use in the cottages. A pastille would burn for about twenty minutes and would have been sufficient to scent an average room. In the nineteenth century the new idea of having a beautiful cottage smoking in the room would have appealed to all classes. Every shape

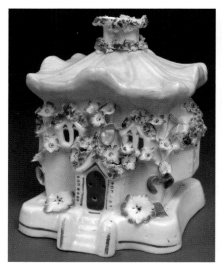

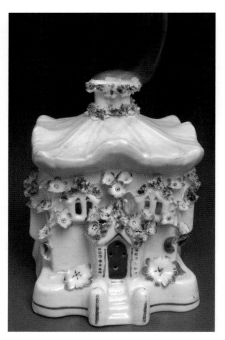

Above: *A small, square country house, c.1835, with upturned coloured roof and Gothic windows. By an unknown maker. (H 14.5, W 11, D 12.)*
Right: *The same pastille burner with a pastille burning inside and smoke escaping.*

Below left: *An unmarked, brightly coloured cottage, c.1840, by Dudson, showing details such as the tiles and standing on three green bun feet. (H 12.5, W 9, D 9.)*

Below right: *A two-storey pagoda, c.1835, by Dudson. (H 16.5, W 14.5, D 14.)*

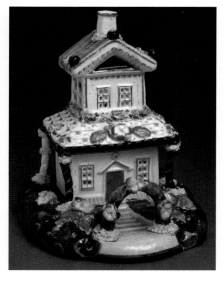

A thatched cottage, c.1830, with a slide for the pastille and probably by Coalport. (H 11, W 13.5, D 11.5.)

of pastille burner produced a different effect, depending upon how the draught was designed. The Dudson 'timbered' cottages standing on their bun feet, with their large chimneys, were spectacular as the smoke could clearly be seen against the bright colours of the cottage. In the bigger cottages two or more pastilles would have been used. Some pastille burners had a slide that carried the pastille.

It was the practice at this time for the gentry to carry pomanders, which they held to their noses as they walked in the smelly streets. Large numbers of pomanders were sold by apothecaries, who claimed they warded off diseases. Today we think of a pomander as

A cottage, c.1825, with a slide in which to put the pastille. (H 11, W 13.5, D 11.5.)

A rare cottage, c.1820 (left), with a specially rounded cup in the base (below), ideal for pastilles or pomanders. The cream rectangular house has a brown thatched roof and is marked 'Flight Barr & Barr Worcester'. (H 17, W 19, D 18.)

Some of the many ingredients from which pastilles and pomanders were made.

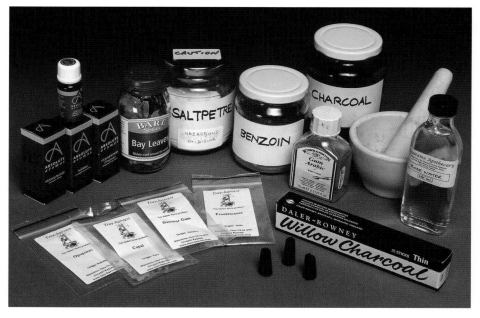

an orange covered with cloves, rubbed with essential oils, wrapped in tissue paper and stored in a dry place for two months. In the late eighteenth century, however, the fashion was to contain the balled pomanders in ornate silver and gold cases. Their original purpose was medicinal as their scent was thought to be effective against insects, plague, epilepsy and colic. Some pomanders induced sleep as they contained hemlock or opium. By the late 1770s they fell out of favour. However, Victorian ladies enjoyed making their own perfumed accessories, including pomander bead necklaces. A pomander perfumed the room for much longer than a pastille and could be easily replaced.

A modern pastille burner adapted from an old Indian design in the form of a lotus flower which holds a scented charcoal cone.

The pastille burner fully open, with the charcoal block to which the essential oils are added.

The manufacturers

By the 1820s many pottery manufacturers realised there was a lucrative market in supplying pastille burners to their middle- and upper-class customers. From surviving evidence it seems that the Alcock and Dudson potteries were the main suppliers. Major potteries such as Chamberlains of Worcester, Spode, Coalport, Minton and Derby produced a limited range, many probably for special orders.

Few pastille burners are marked with the factory back stamp, which may indicate that some were made as sample pieces and exhibited in the pottery's showrooms. Documentary evidence is scarce and a true attribution to each pottery difficult. However, after study of the prevailing market conditions related to each pottery's market share, the quality of the product, and the design, decoration and variation of ceramic colour, it is possible to identify some makes reliably and to provide possible attributions for many more.

SAMUEL ALCOCK

The Samuel Alcock Hill Top pottery at Burslem in Staffordshire made examples of all the varying styles of pastille burners, including tollhouses, churches, cottages, small houses and lodges, in varying sizes. They are finely potted and tastefully decorated with applied

(Left) A tollhouse, sometimes called an umbrella house, by Alcock, c.1830, impressed number 84. (H 9, W 7, D 8.) (Right) A smaller model by Alcock, c.1830, impressed number 85. (H 8, W 6, D 7.)

Above left: *A rare lavender cottage by Alcock, c.1830; unmarked. (H 13.5, W 17, D 12.5.)*
Above right: *A two-storey lavender house by Alcock, c.1830; unmarked. (H 11, W 11.5, D 11.)*

flowers and are brightly painted and gilded. The pagodas and temples are often more ornate than the cottages. Many models were produced not only in white porcelain but also in a distinctive lavender colour.

Samuel Alcock (1799–1848), despite having no family potting connections, became a highly successful pottery manufacturer. No

Below left: *A violet blue house by Alcock with gables and bay windows, c.1830; unmarked. (H 13, W 13.5, D 10.)*
Below right: *A lavender house by Alcock, c.1830; unmarked. Note the umbrella extension at one end. (H 15, W 12.5, D 14.)*

Above left: *A mansion by Alcock, c.1835. (H 13, W 16.5, D 13.) Alcock also produced a similar model in white only.*
Above right: *A fine example of a coloured tollhouse by Alcock; impressed number 83. (H 13, W 11, D 10.)*

Above: *Tollhouses by Alcock showing different style roofs. Left, impressed number 80; right, number 81. (Left, H 20, W 12.5, D 12.5; right, H 17, W 11.5, D 11.5.)*

A white lodge cottage by Alcock, c.1825. (H 12.5, W 14, D 12.)

A lavender Georgian-style house by Alcock, c.1825; marked with pattern number 1/232. (H 14, W 16, D 13.)

doubt the business expertise he learnt from his uncle Joseph Locker, a grocer, tea dealer, provision dealer, chandler and banker, and his choice of business associates were the secrets of his success. In 1839 he rebuilt and extended the Hill (or Hill Top) pottery at the junction of Westport Road and Greenhead Street in Burslem. Alcock's new pottery was an impressive building designed on a Venetian theme. It was completed in November and a party was held at the George

Below left: *A large lavender castle by Alcock, c.1830. There are no marks. The piece is reminiscent of Warwick Castle. (H 19, W 18, D 15.5.)*

Below right: *A rare white two-storey house by Alcock, c.1830; unmarked. The design is usually seen in lavender. (H 15, W 12.5, D 14.)*

Above: *A lavender three-steepled tollhouse by Alcock, c.1835; unmarked. (H 15,W 14, D 11.)* Left: *The same three-steepled tollhouse was also made in white, Alcock, c.1835; unmarked.*

Hotel, Burslem, to celebrate, followed by a Grand Ball held on 10th June 1840, attended by over two hundred guests, who danced to the Duke of Sutherland's Quadrille Band. Alcock's were now producing a full range of tea and dinner ware, jugs, Parian figures and pastille burners, and by 1842 were employing four hundred workers. Unlike many of their other productions, no pastille burners have been found marked with a factory back stamp though many are impressed with a number and some show pattern numbers. The following impressed numbers have been found, which tie in with the numbering system known to have been used by Alcock from shards found on the site: 4, 6, 8, 13, 18, 19, 38, 39, 49, 56, 61, 78, 79, 80, 81, 82, 83, 85, 125, 132, 134, 135, 154, 155, 260, 306, 324. Pattern numbers marked in puce are examples of the 1/series: 1/1325, 1/2382 and 1/2444; other puce numbers found are 1605 and 1797.

DUDSON

Richard Dudson, the founder of the Dudson potteries, was born in 1768. He trained as a potter and colour-maker and in 1800 started his own business at Broad Street, Shelton, Stoke-on-Trent. However, it was his eldest son, Thomas, born in 1786 and trained by his father, who established the pottery at Hope Street, Hanley,

A large violet blue lodge by Dudson with a slide for the pastille, c.1830; unmarked. (H 11,W 12, D 12.5.)

producing figures and a large range of pastille burners. Fortunately an 1842 factory order book has survived which shows the range.

Cottages

Flower cottages 10/6 a dozen
Blue cottages 15/6 a dozen
Swiss cottages 9/- a dozen
White and gold cottages 10/- a dozen

Earthenware Cottages

Round 5/- & 3/- a dozen
New 5/6 a dozen
Thatched 5/6 a dozen
Blue Thatched 5/6 a dozen

Although some castles are known they are not listed here, but Chinese temples selling at ten and eighteen shillings a dozen are. Dudson timbered cottages are easily recognisable, because shards, now exhibited at the Dudson Museum at Hope Street, Hanley, have been found on the old factory site and prove that hitherto unidentified cottage shapes were manufactured by the Dudson

A thatched, timbered cottage by Dudson. (H 12.5, W 11.5, D 13.)

Above: *An octagonal summerhouse by Dudson, c. 1830. (H 13, W 12, D 10.)*

A double-fronted cottage, c. 1830, attributed to Dudson. (H 11, W 13, D 8.5.)

pottery. The cottages are unique, being decorated in bright vibrant colours, very different from those used by the other potteries of the period, and the designs are varied and exciting. Nearly all of these thatched cottages stand on bun feet and have large ventilation holes in their base. When the pastille is lit the perfumed smoke pours from their chimneys. The market for making pastille burners in which medicinal pastilles could be burnt would have appealed to Dudson's, as surviving recipes show that the Dudson family was interested in recipes for troublesome coughs and 'opening medicines', among other ailments.

Thomas Dudson was very successful; he would have regarded marking his merchandise

(Left) A lavender octagonal keep or dovecote by Alcock, c.1830. (H 13.5, W 12.5, D 12.5.) (Right) This blue dovecote by Dudson, c.1830, is made from blue clay, which exactly matches shards on display in the Dudson Museum. It shows a great attention to detail, having the tiles marked out carefully on the roof, and is similar in design to many dovecotes found on country estates. (H 13.5, W 12.5, D 12.5.)

as an unnecessary expense because he was able to sell all he produced. With no identifying mark, Dudson's porcelain cottages are difficult to attribute. What gives them away as Dudson's is their palette, as Dudson's cottages and figures are decorated with distinctive bright and vibrant colours, unlike any other products of the period.

In comparison with the Alcock pottery Dudson's was small, but he saw the same marketing opportunity. Thomas Dudson himself designed the cottages, having the ability to make his ware stand out in the market place. He competed with Alcock by producing a large range of distinctive blue cottages.

When Thomas Dudson died in 1845 the business was continued by his son James (1812–82). Potter, colour-maker and property dealer, James exhibited figures at the Great Exhibition of 1851 and was listed in the exhibition catalogue as 'Dudson J., Hope Street, Hanley, Staffordshire, Manufacture ornamental china figures'. He exhibited again in the London Exhibition of

An ornate picturesque cottage, c.1830–50, attributed to Dudson; unmarked. (H 11, W 9, D 9.)

A typical small square cottage, c.1830–50, attributed to Dudson. Note the bun feet and bright colours. (H 9, W 7, D 7.)

1862, then listed as 'Dudson, James, Hanley, Improved ironstone jugs and teapots with metal tops, stone candlesticks, ornamental china figures'. Toys and figures were made by Richard Dudson and his youngest son, also Richard, at the Broad Street pottery and, from 1839, at a third pottery in Cannon Street, Shelton. Both these potteries closed in 1843 and unfortunately no examples of the ware they produced have so far been identified. It is not known when the production of Dudson pastille burners ceased.

WORCESTER

As there were three rival potteries in Worcester in the early nineteenth century identification of Worcester pastille burners and night-lights can be difficult, although a few marked examples do provide an excellent guide. The Worcester potteries supplied the aristocracy and upper end of the market. They all produced highly decorated and complicated designs, which are distinctive; the colour palette is tasteful, not garish. The smaller cottages re-create realistic country estate cottages or summerhouses, while the Swiss cottages or lodges are larger and more complex.

Flight Barr & Barr, 1813–40

The pottery at Warmstry House, situated on the banks of the river Severn, was founded by Dr John Wall and later became known as

Back and front views of a rare Worcester cottage, clearly marked with the impressed crown and 'Flight Barr & Barr Worcester' in puce and impressed FBB. (H 16.5, W 27, D 18.)

The Royal China Manufactory. Thomas Flight took it over in 1783. He and his sons, Joseph and John, ran the pottery, initially with great difficulty, but after a visit from George III, from whom they obtained a prestigious order and the Royal Warrant, their fortunes changed. They opened a shop and warehouse at 1 Coventry Street, London, and had a retail shop in the High Street at Worcester.

In 1792, after the deaths of Thomas and John, Joseph Flight took into partnership Martin Barr, and they traded as Flight & Barr. After 1800 they produced pastille burners and night-lights, the first of the Worcester pieces. In 1813 Martin Barr, Joseph Flight and Martin's surviving sons, George and Martin, continued the pottery productions, trading as Flight Barr & Barr. By the early 1830s the pottery was struggling to survive and, when Joseph Flight died in 1838, the Barr brothers amalgamated with their successful rival, Chamberlains. Examples of Flight Barr & Barr pastille burners are rare.

Chamberlains, 1786–1851

Robert Chamberlain (1737–98) learnt the art of potting at Dr Wall's pottery, which he left in the 1780s to start his own decorating business in King Street, St Peter's, Worcester, with his son Humphrey. Eventually they started to produce their own pottery and porcelain in the Diglis area of Worcester and opened a shop at 33 High Street, in direct competition with the Flight Barr & Barr pottery.

Chamberlains produced both conical and elaborate burners, which they called pastille burners, but which other potteries marketed as incense burners. They were of the highest quality, finely

Left: *A grand mansion, c.1825. This very rare two-storey house has an elaborate gilt roof and is marked 'Chamberlain Worcester' in red on the pastille slide. (H 14, W 16, D 16.)*

Right: *The mansion's slide clearly marked with the factory mark.*

gilt with fine hand-painting. Chamberlains produced a small but exquisitely designed range, which only the aristocracy and wealthy middle class could have afforded.

The Chamberlain records of July 1791 refer to houses or toy houses but in 1813 a house for pastilles is shown. These houses were very expensive, costing fourteen shillings, whereas the cottages were only six shillings. By 1820 thatched cottages in white and gold with thatched covers were ten shillings. Chamberlains had obviously recognised the potential of the middle-class market with these ranges and yet still catered for the wealthy, as a three-chimney house in 1829 in their Bond Street shop was quoted at £1 11s 6d. Their

A small farm labourer's house, c.1825, marked 'Chamberlain Worcester' in red. (H 8.5, W 8, D 8.)

A small Worcester cottage, c. 1825. The mound base has an unusual centre into which the top fits and is held in place by a small lip. (H 7.5, W 7, D 7.)

gazebo or summerhouse range is very different, having much longer chimneys than the Coalport and Spode versions. They also produced a biscuit (unglazed) version of a lodge house, which must have formed an excellent variation in their range. Whether any of these fine lodges were replicas of real estate buildings has never been proved.

The final range produced was the beehive cottage, so called because of a beehive feature on the side of the house; some have a

Worcester beehive cottages, c. 1830; unmarked. (Left, H 14.5, W 9, D 9; right, H 13, W 9, D 9.)

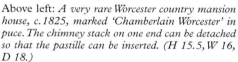

Above left: *A very rare Worcester country mansion house, c.1825, marked 'Chamberlain Worcester' in puce. The chimney stack on one end can be detached so that the pastille can be inserted. (H 15.5, W 16, D 18.)*

Above right: *A very rare Worcester gazebo, marked 'Chamberlain Worcester' in red. The roof is supported by eight columns surrounding the octagonal gazebo. (H 13.5, W 13, D 13.)*

Right: *A beehive cottage, c.1830; unmarked but possibly Worcester. (H 14.5, W 9.5, D 9.5.)*

variation with a lady looking out of the window. All are beautifully hand-painted and decorated with great taste, no doubt designed by Humphrey and his sons, Humphrey and Walter, who were both fine artists.

Thomas Grainger & Company, 1805–99

George Grainger was apprenticed to Samuel Bradley as a painter. He was a relation by marriage of the Chamberlains. In 1805 his son, Thomas, started the third pottery in Worcester, in the Blockhouse area in St Martin's Gate and George Street. Although it is well documented that the company made pot lids to cover Muroma fragrant pomade for the hair, there is only one reference to a night-light and none to pastille burners. There is little doubt, however, that a small range would have been made, but direct attribution is not yet

A rare turquoise pagoda, c.1835. This piece was once thought to be by Grainger of Worcester but this provenance is now doubtful. (H 16,W 16, D 13.)

possible. The company was also known simply as Grainger & Company.

SPODE

Josiah Spode II (1755–1827) of the Spode pottery, Stoke-on-Trent, Staffordshire, was an astute businessman who had inherited a flourishing pottery. He and William Copeland had run the London showroom with great success. Keeping in touch with changing fashions and marketing trends, he initially produced a small, simple pastille burner in the

Left: *A Spode Swiss cottage, c.1825, marked 'Spode Felspar porcelain'. (H 14,W 24, D 24.)*

Below left: *A Spode gazebo, c.1820, marked 'Spode Felspar porcelain'. (H 17.5,W 13, D 13.)*

Below right: *A gazebo or summerhouse, c.1820; unmarked but possibly by Spode. (H 12.5,W 12, D 12.)*

shape of a house. However, by 1825, in view of the competition from the Worcester potteries, and using the new Felspar body invented in 1820, he produced a Swiss cottage and three gazebos, which he marked with the Felspar mark. The colouring is distinctive – a warm yellow and brown with gilded white leaves. These pastille burners appealed to his wealthy customers. The mould of the simple country house was adapted and used in 1850 when W. T. Copeland (who bought the Spode pottery and business in 1833) produced Shakespeare's Cottage in their Parian range.

WEDGWOOD

The Wedgwood archives show that they made cottages, but whether they were ever used to burn pastilles is not so far proven. However, outline drawings in the Number One shape book and the 'Useful and Ornamental Ware' price book look like cottages, but as they are entered in the middle of designs for ornamental flowerpots the evidence is confusing. Brown and green glazed cottages and even a pearlware enamelled variety are shown but to date no examples have been found to help solve this fascinating puzzle.

LEEDS

One early gazebo made by the Leeds pottery has been identified but examples are generally rare. Pastille burners have been found with the impressed mark 'LEEDS POTTERY', in a straight line. The mark is very misleading, however, as this straight mark reveals they were produced in the early twentieth century. The early Leeds

Above: *A small biscuit cottage, c.1900, impressed 'LEEDS'. (H 9,W 7.5, D 8.)*

Left: *A gazebo, c.1830; unmarked but a similar piece by the Leeds pottery is known. (H 13,W 12, D 12.)*

(Left) A small Coalport cottage, c.1830, marked 'CD' in blue. (H 11, W 13.5, D 11.5.) (Inset) The base of the Coalport cottage, with the clear 'CD' marks.

mark is curved, with the letters heavier at the top than at the bottom. Beware of imitations of pastille burners with a hole at the back but no opening in the chimneys, made by Seniors at Leeds in the early twentieth century. Mr Senior, in an interview in 1967, said that several flower-encrusted cottages were made; they were enamelled and fitted with a sliding door to function as incense burners.

COALPORT

John Rose, who ran the Coalport pottery, was described as 'a man of wonderful energy, being strong in body, having a clear head, and a cool judgment, and gifted with remarkable perseverance'. He never missed a business opportunity. Although in the 1820s and 1830s the company produced some cottage pastille burners (as marked examples are known), Coalport preferred to cater for the upper-class market by providing vase-shaped pastille burners. The best-known pastille burner is a gazebo, clearly marked 'CD' and similar to those produced by Spode but designed with a smaller base. Coalport also produced a church and an arbour, reproduced in different colours. Their range for the collectors' market is

An unmarked white church, c.1825, possibly by Coalport. (H 14, W 14.5, D 10.)

Above: *A summer pavilion, c.1825, by Coalport with 'CD' marked in blue. (H 12, W 11, D 11.)*

Right: *A round house, c.1820–5, marked with the Bloore Derby mark in red. (H 14, W 11.5, D 11.5.)*

comprehensive; some of the old moulds were used to produce limited editions in the 1990s, and they also produced a new range of models for the Millennium. They are no longer in production.

DERBY

Derby pastille burners *c.*1825 are rare but marked examples have been found. The colour palette, basically variants of cream and moss green, is different from that of any other maker. Likewise the design of the base, with a sloping recessed pierced centre, is unique.

A timbered cottage, c.1861, marked 'Stevenson & Hancock Derby'. (H 9, W 8, D 9.)

A Minton dairy, c.1821. Although unmarked, this piece is shown in the Minton pattern book. (H 10, W 10, D 9.)

Stevenson & Hancock of the King Street pottery, Derby, produced a small thatched cottage marked with the red mark, after 1861, but as yet few other Derby examples have emerged.

MINTON

Only two models of Minton pastille burners have been found in the Minton pattern books. One is a dairy in blue and white; another, a very rare example, is of a Roman forum, pattern number 33, based on a design by Decimus Burton in 1828. Also, a castle gatehouse in white and gold as an inkwell is illustrated.

A Minton gatehouse, c.1830. Although unmarked, this piece is shown in the Minton pattern book. (H 10,W 10, D 9.)

Further reading

Black, P. *The Book of Pot Pourri*. In association with the National Trust, 1989.

Clive, K. V. 'Collecting Old China and Pottery Models of Cottages'. *Connoisseur Magazine*, April 1912.

Clive, K. V. 'More about Collecting Antique China and Pottery Houses'. *Connoisseur Magazine*, August 1917.

Darley, G. *Villages of Vision*. Paladin, 1978.

Day, I. *Perfumery with Herbs*. Dana Longman & Todd, 1979.

Devereux, R. 'English Porcelain Pastille Burners, Cottages, Castles, Churches and Others'. A paper read at the Linnean Society Rooms on 20th January 1996 for the English Ceramic Circle.

Guild, R. *The Complete Victorian Housebook Guide*. Sidgwick & Jackson, 1989.

Hansell, P. and J. *Dovecotes*. Shire, second edition 2001.

Hughes, B. 'Cottages to Scent a Room: The Vogue of the Pastille Burner'. *Country Life*, December 1963.

Loudon, J. C. *Encyclopaedia of Cottage, Farm, and Villa Architecture*. Volumes 1 and 2. Donhead Publishing, 2000.

Newman, J. *Candles*. Parkgate Books, 2000.

Somerville-Large, P. *The Irish Country House: A Social History*. Sinclair Stevenson, 1995.

Robinson, H. 'More about China Cottages'. *Connoisseur Magazine*, February 1913.

A large, ornate floral cottage, c.1840; unidentified. (H 15, W 17.5, D 16.5.)

Places to visit

Castle Fraser (National Trust for Scotland), Sauchen, Inverurie, Aberdeenshire AB51 7LD. Telephone: 01330 833463. Website: www.nts.org.uk

The Dudson Museum, Dudson Centre, Hope Street, Hanley, Stoke-on-Trent, Staffordshire ST1 5BS. Telephone: 01782 821075. Website: www.dudson.co.uk

Fenton House (National Trust), Windmill Lane, Hampstead, London NW3 6RT. Telephone: 020 7435 3471. Website: www.nationaltrust.org.uk

Gardiner Museum of Ceramic Art, 60 McCaul Street, Toronto, Ontario, Canada M5T 1V9. Telephone: (001) 416 586 8080. Website: www.gardinermuseum.on.ca

The Potteries Museum and Art Gallery, Bethesda Street, Hanley, Stoke-on-Trent, Staffordshire ST1 3DW. Telephone: 01782 232323. Website: www2002.stoke.gov.uk/museums

The Victoria and Albert Museum, Cromwell Road, South Kensington, London SW7 2RL. Telephone: 020 7942 2000. Website: www.vam.ac.uk

The Wedgwood Museum, Barlaston, Stoke-on-Trent, Staffordshire ST12 9ES. Telephone: 01782 282818. Website: www.wedgwoodmuseum.org.uk

The Worcester Porcelain Museum, Severn Street, Worcester WR1 2NE. Telephone: 01905 746000. Website: www.worcesterporcelainmuseum.org.uk

A pottery house, c.1849; unmarked but probably by Alcock. (H 15, W 12.5, D 14.)

Index